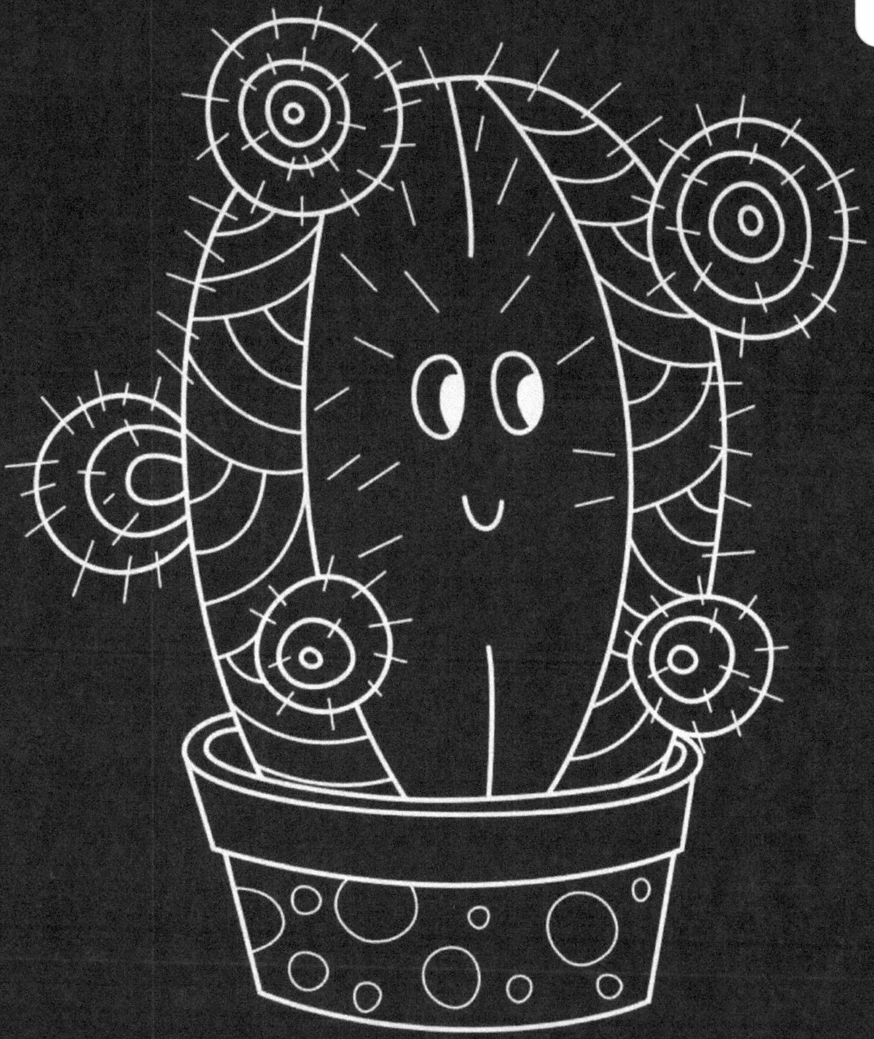

TINY CACTUS PUBLISHING

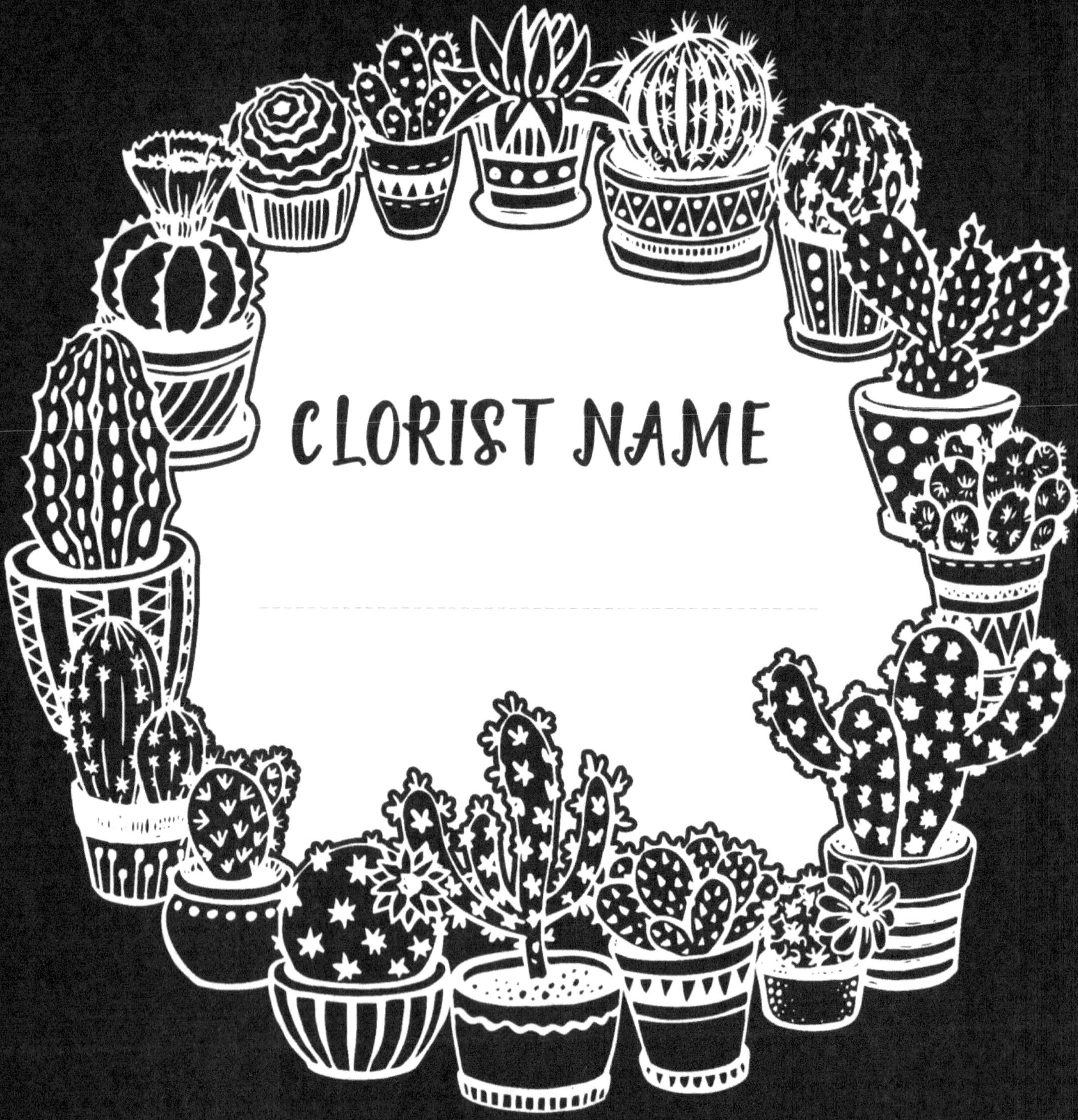
CLORIST NAME

TEST PAGE

PREPARE YOUR COLOR

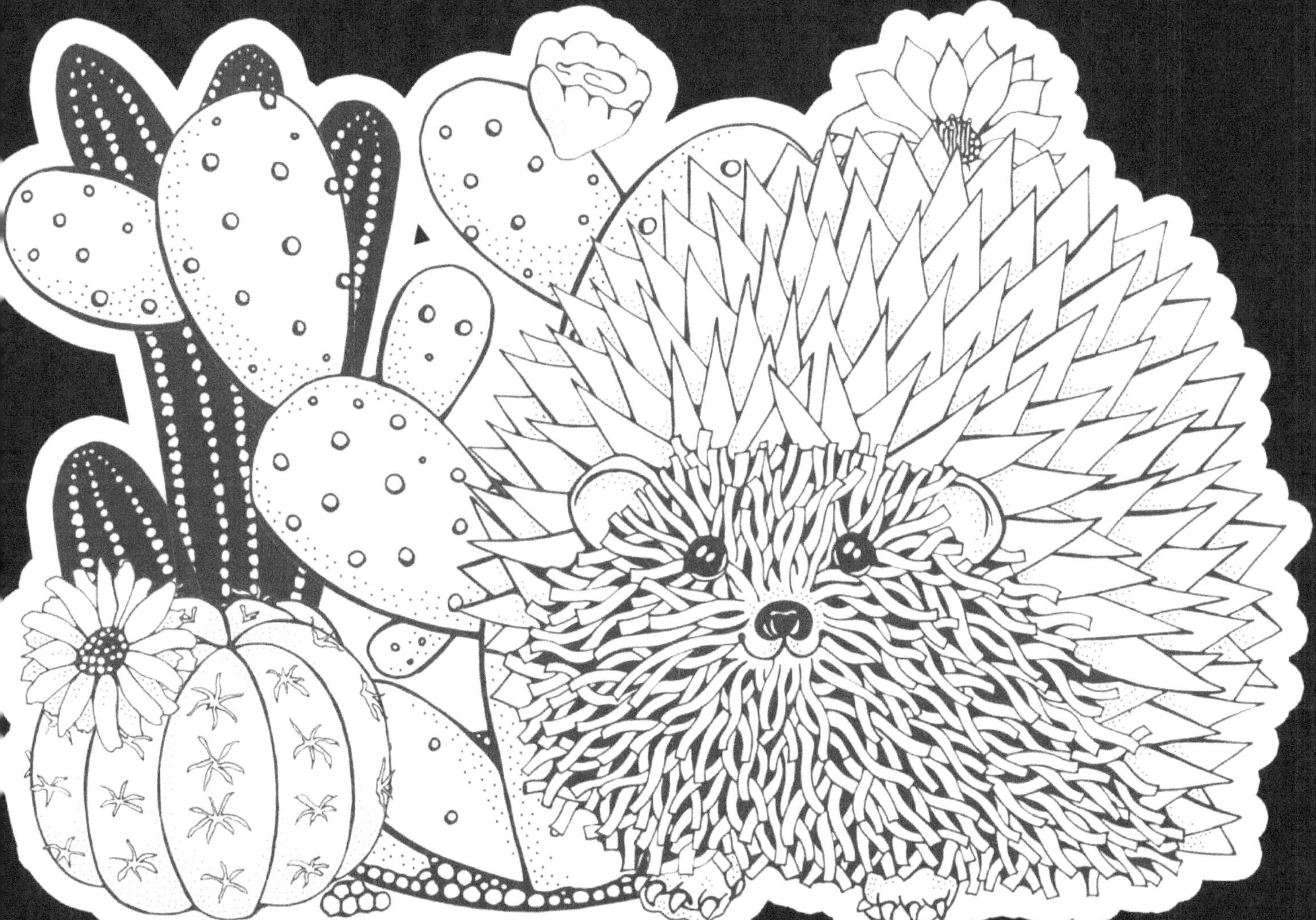

WARM UP !!

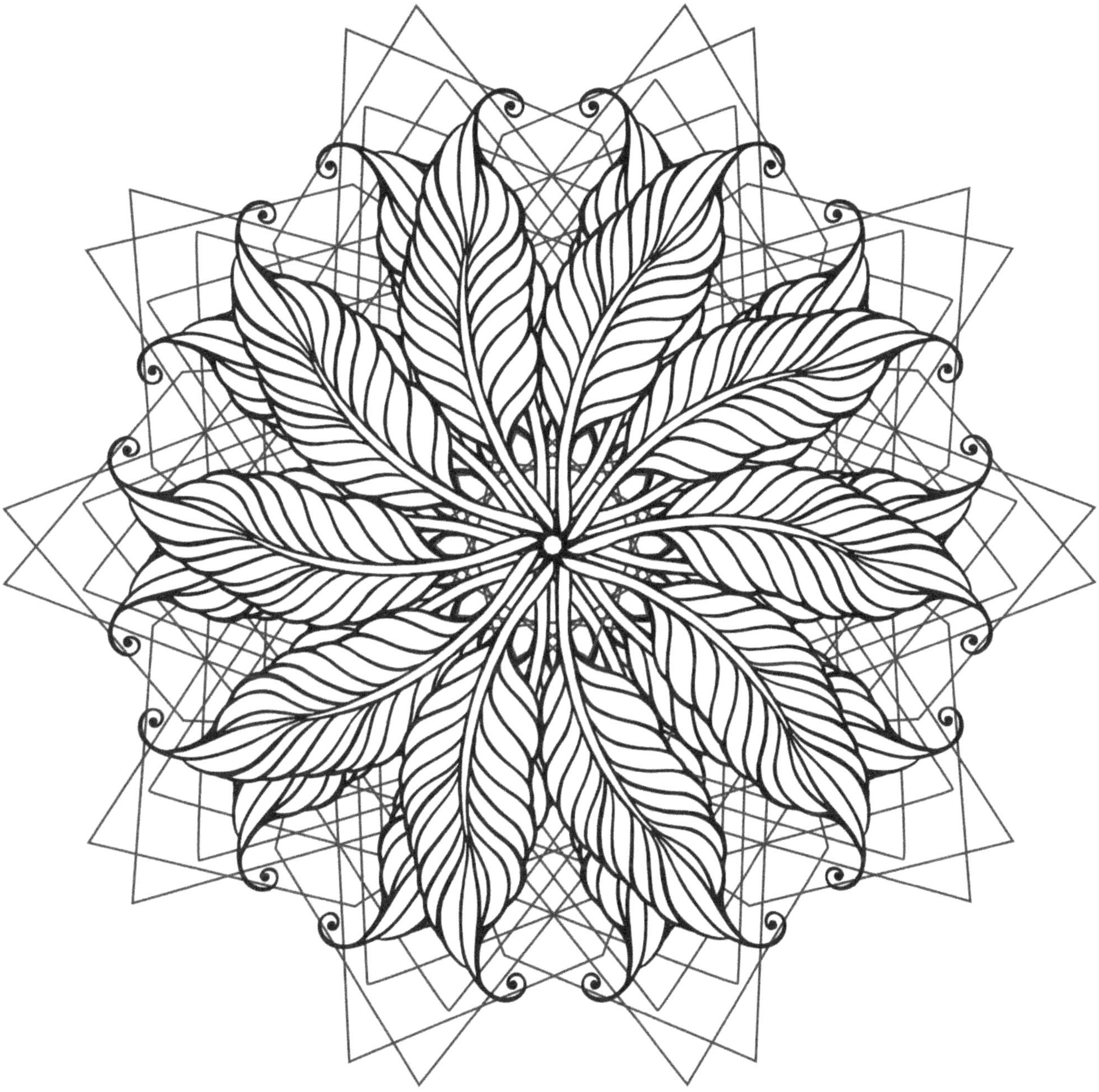

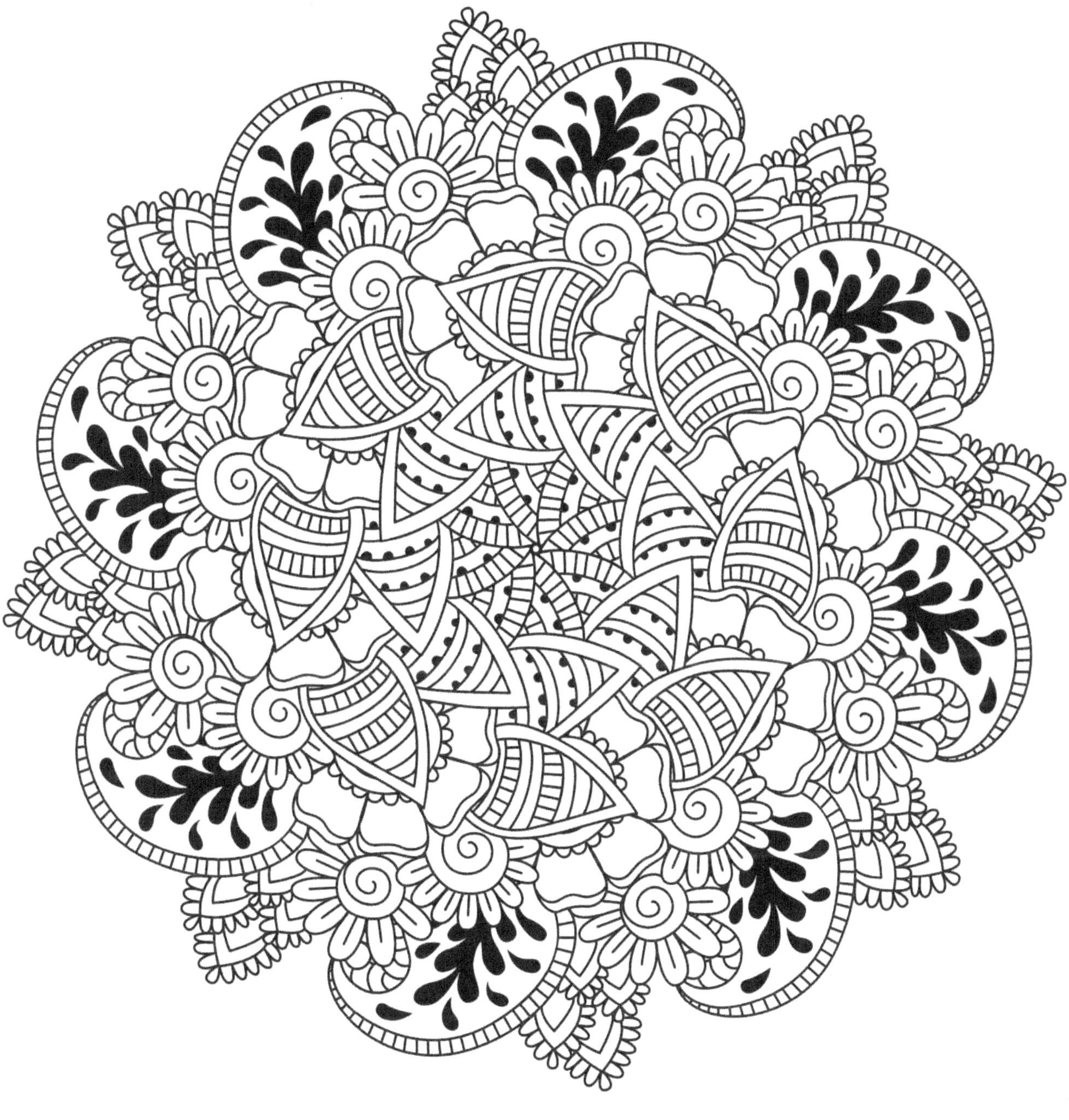

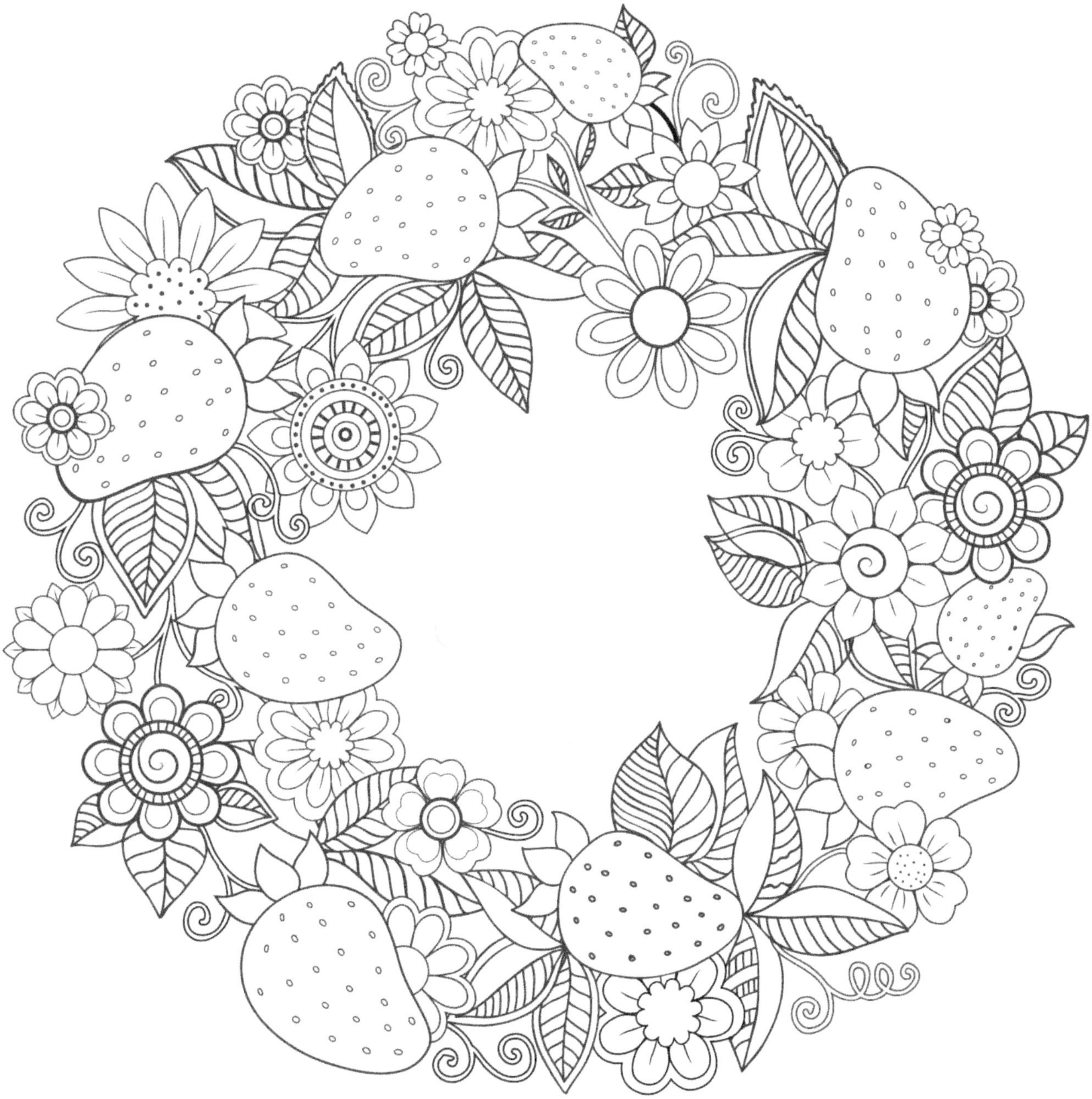

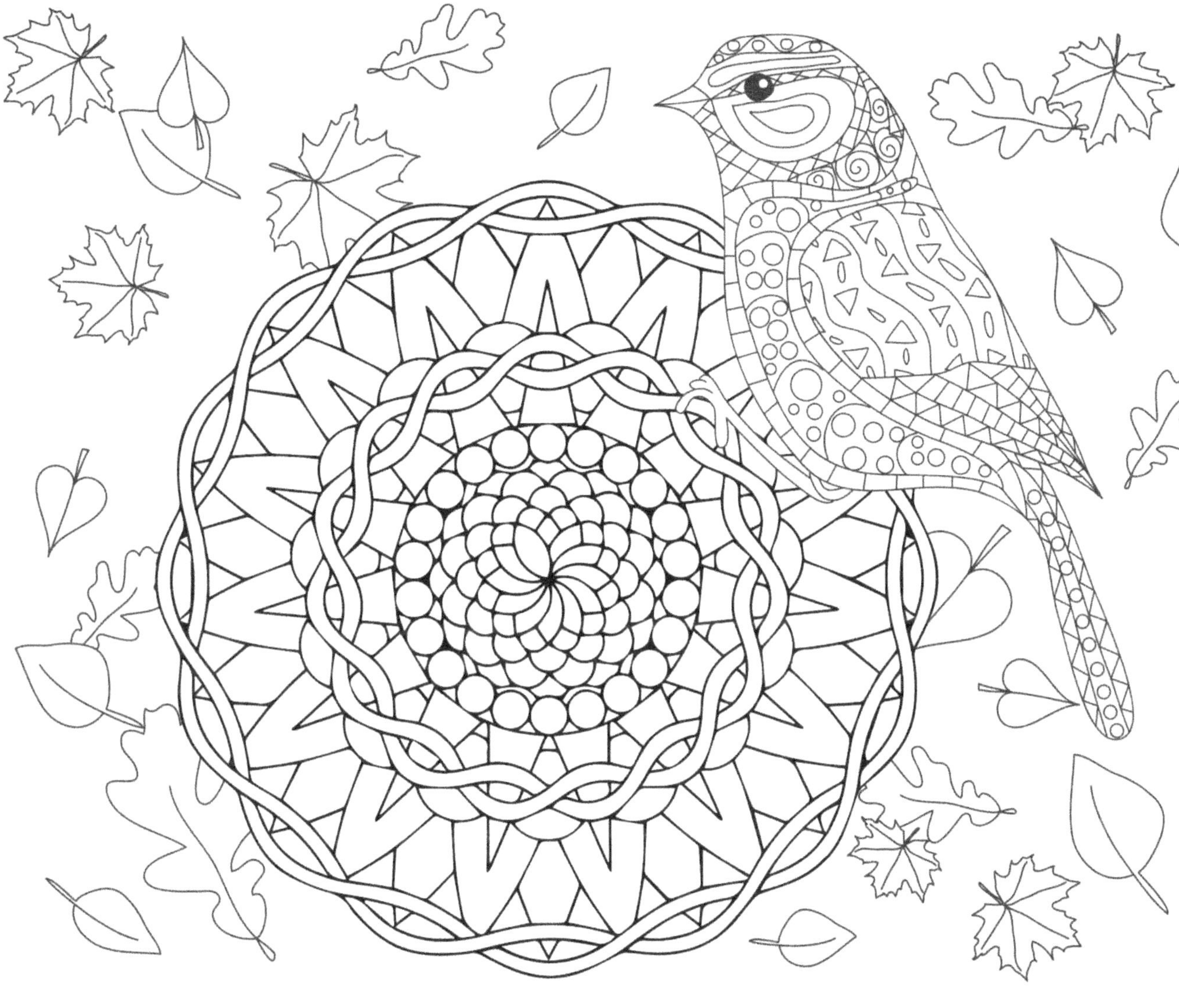

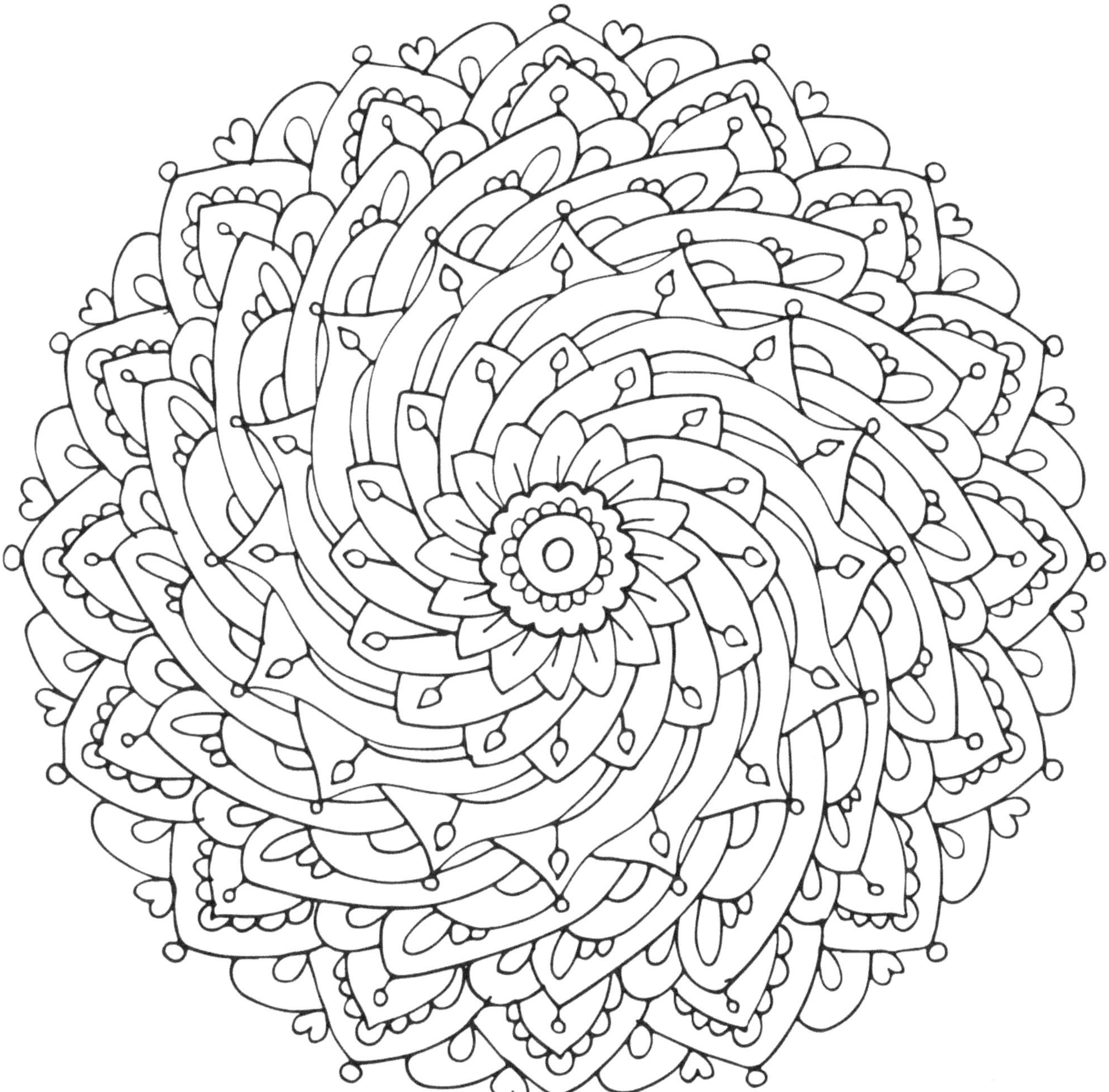

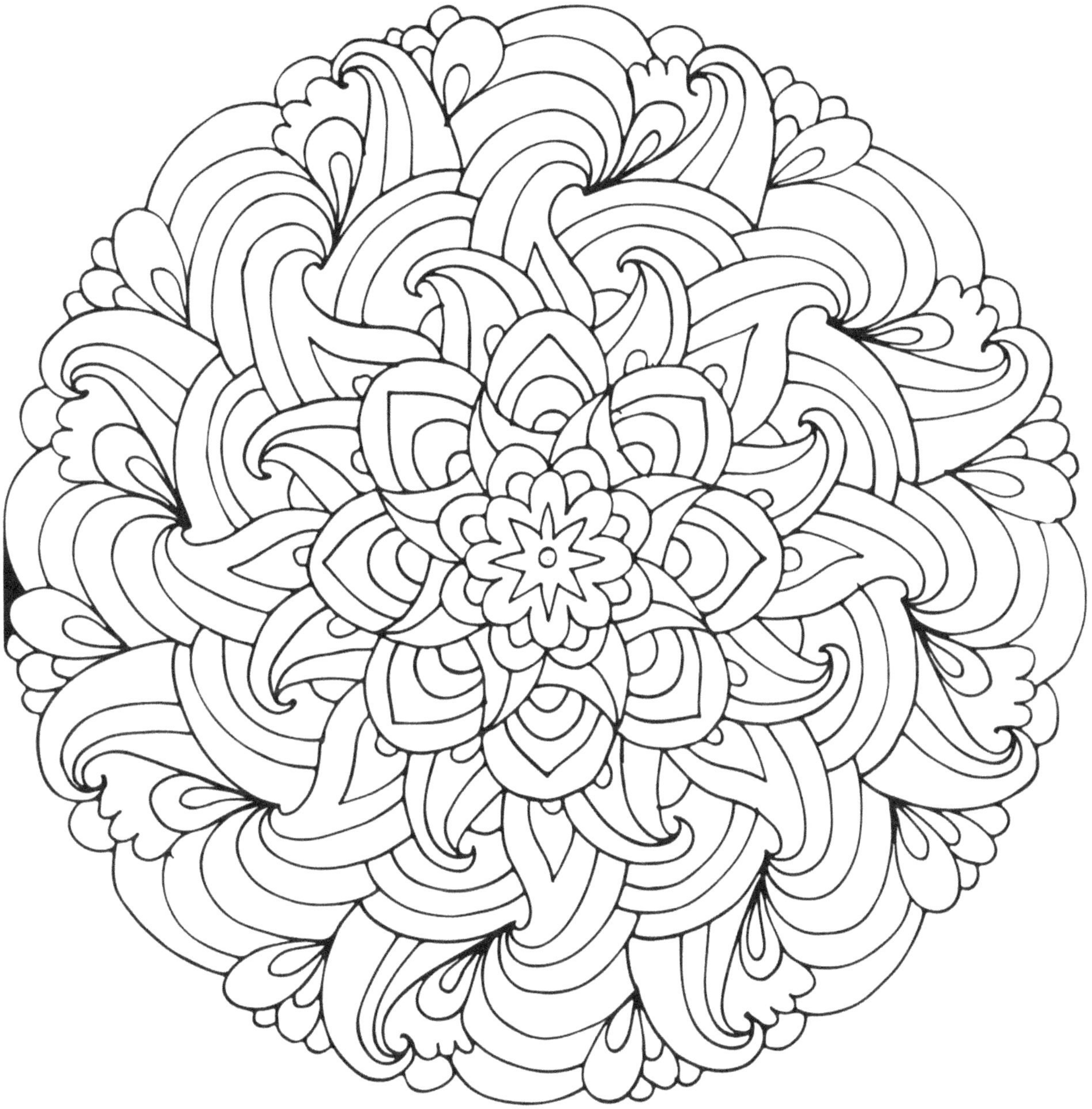

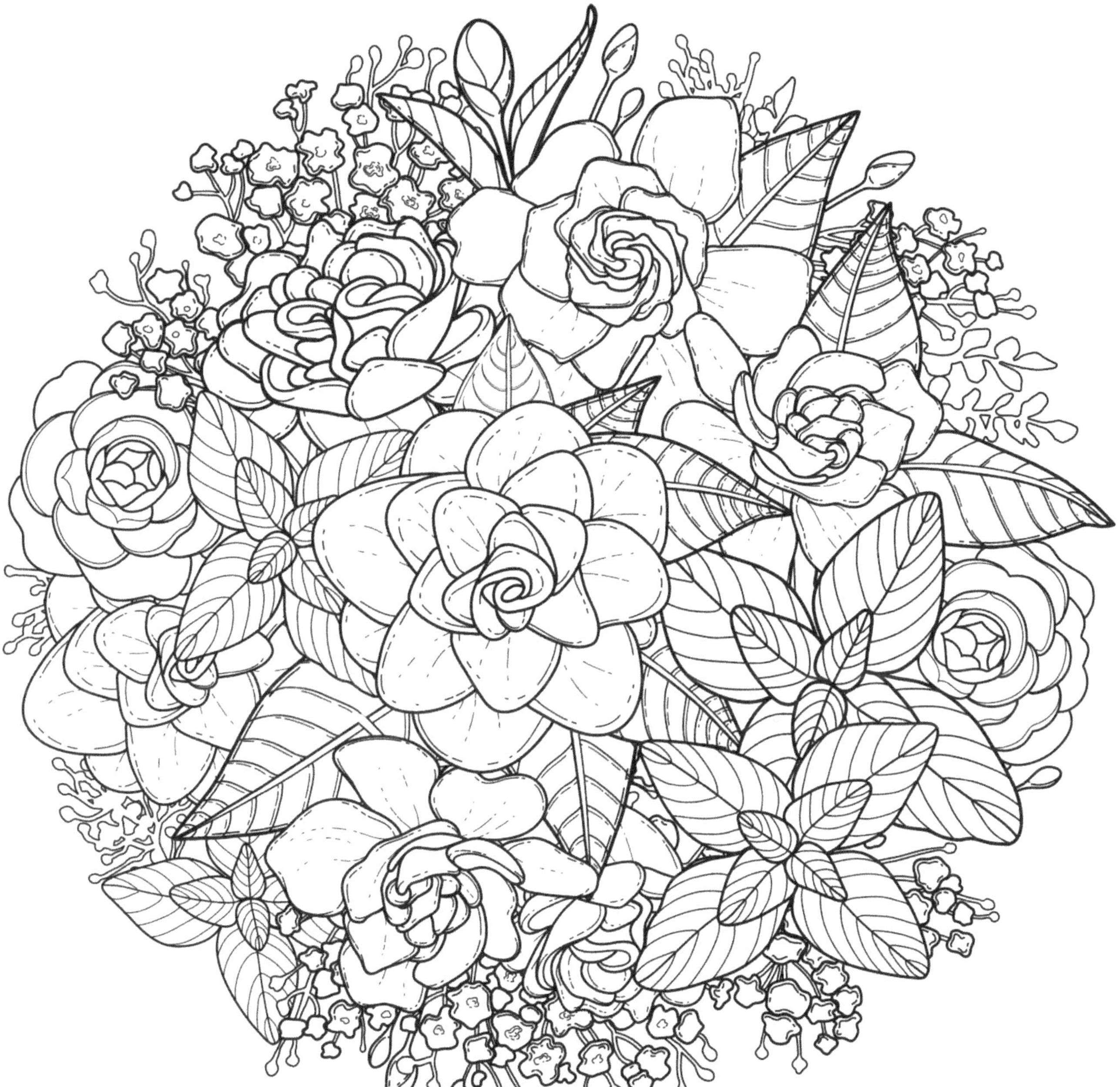

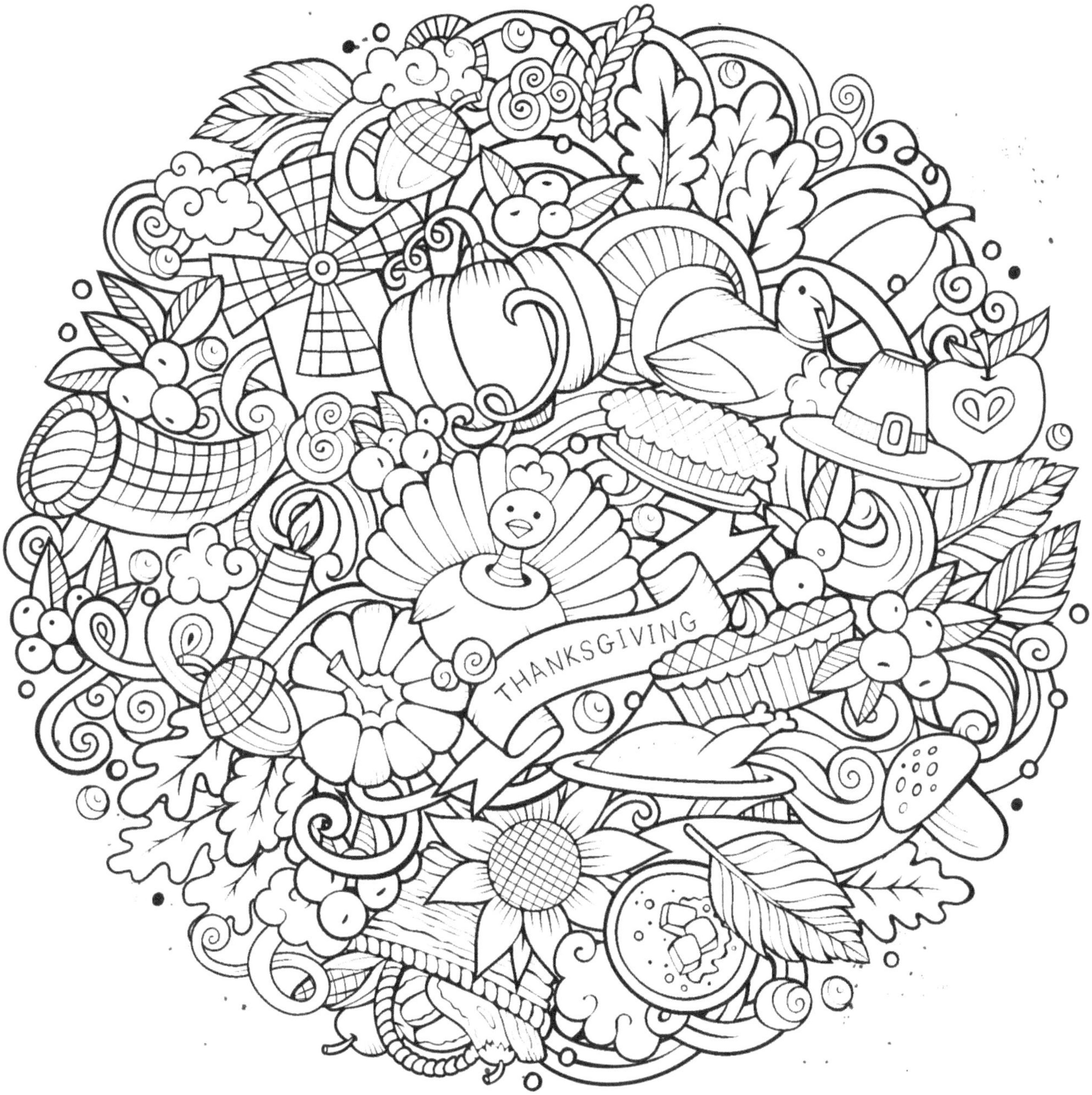
THANKSGIVING

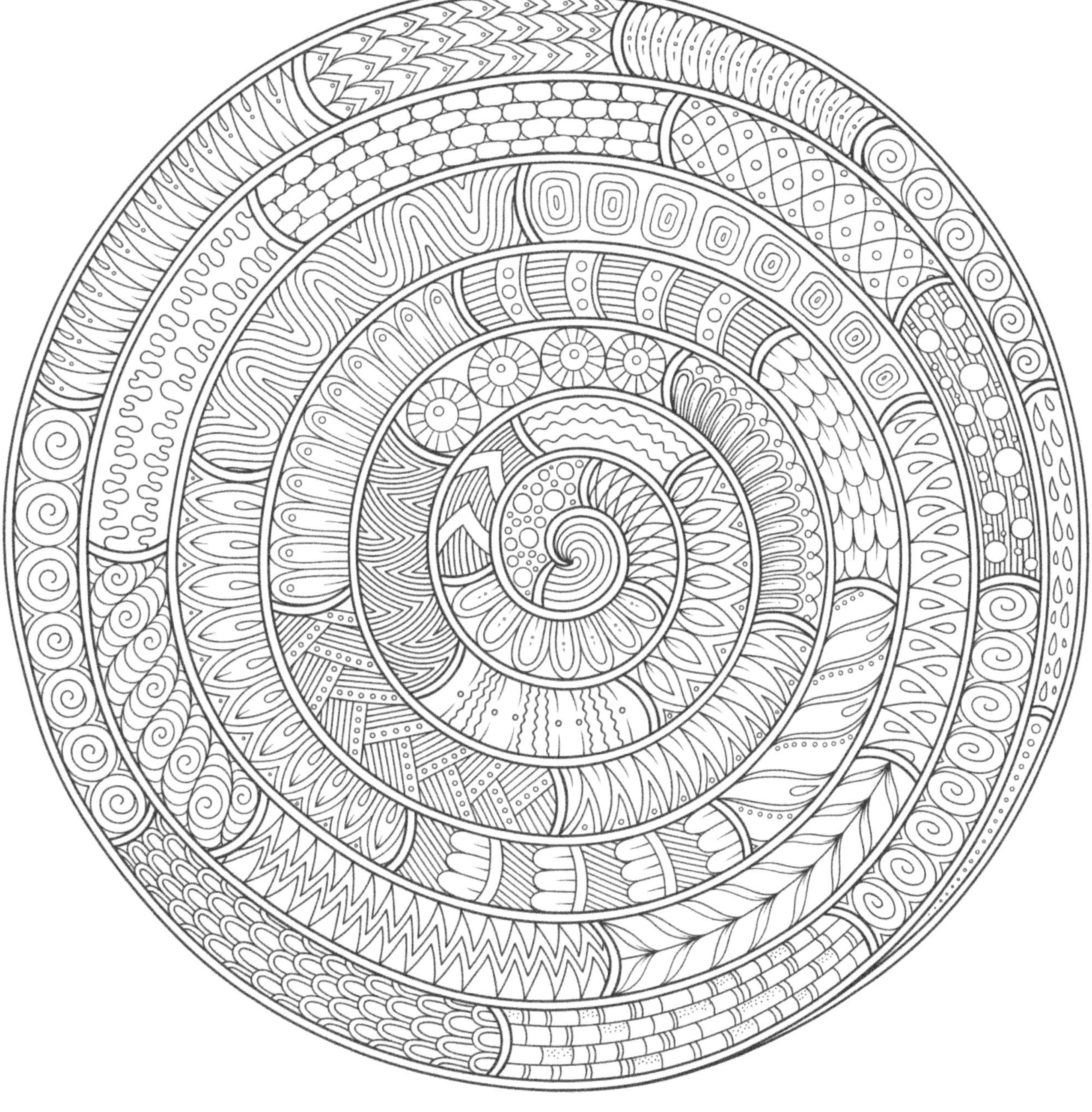

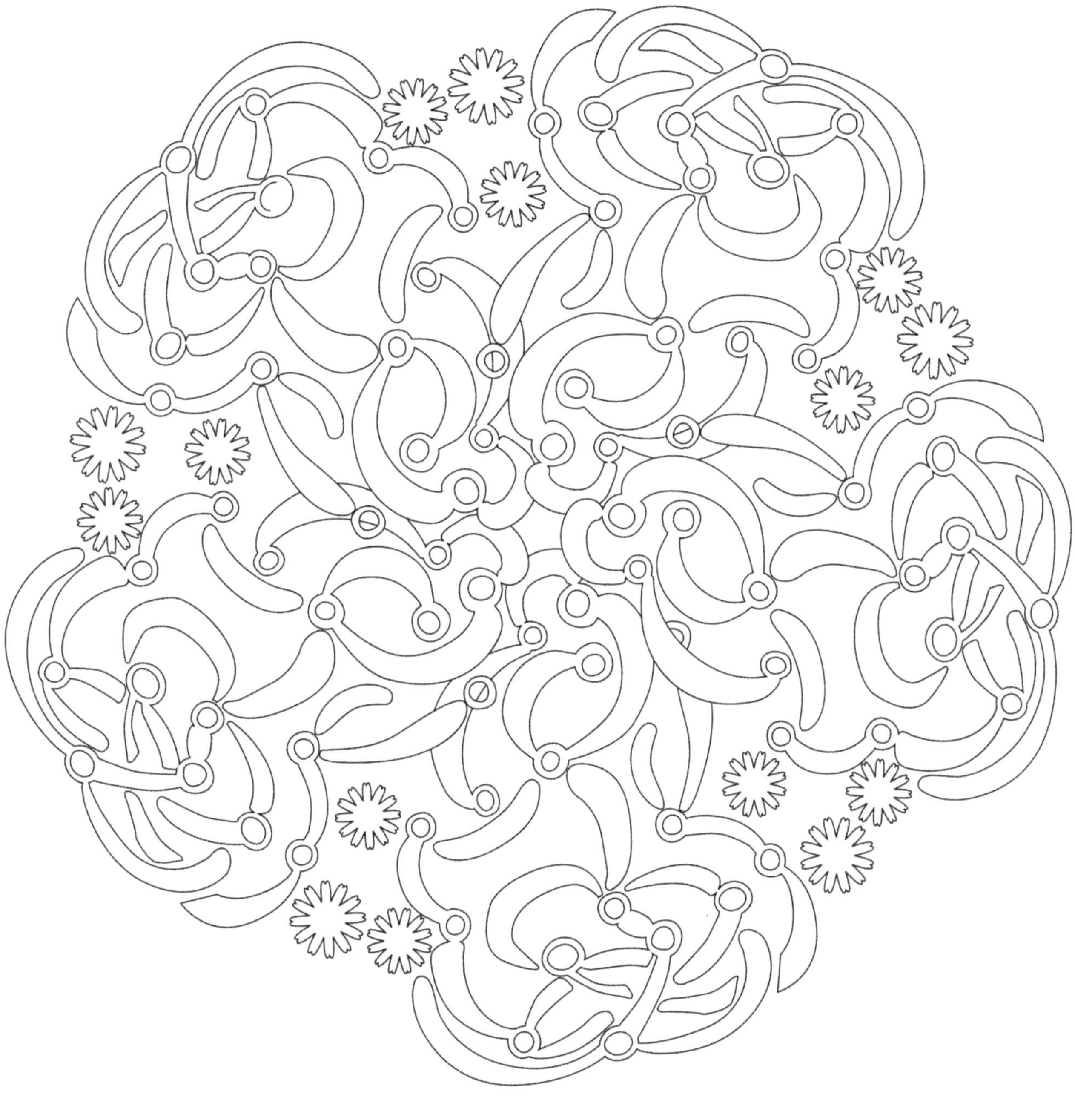

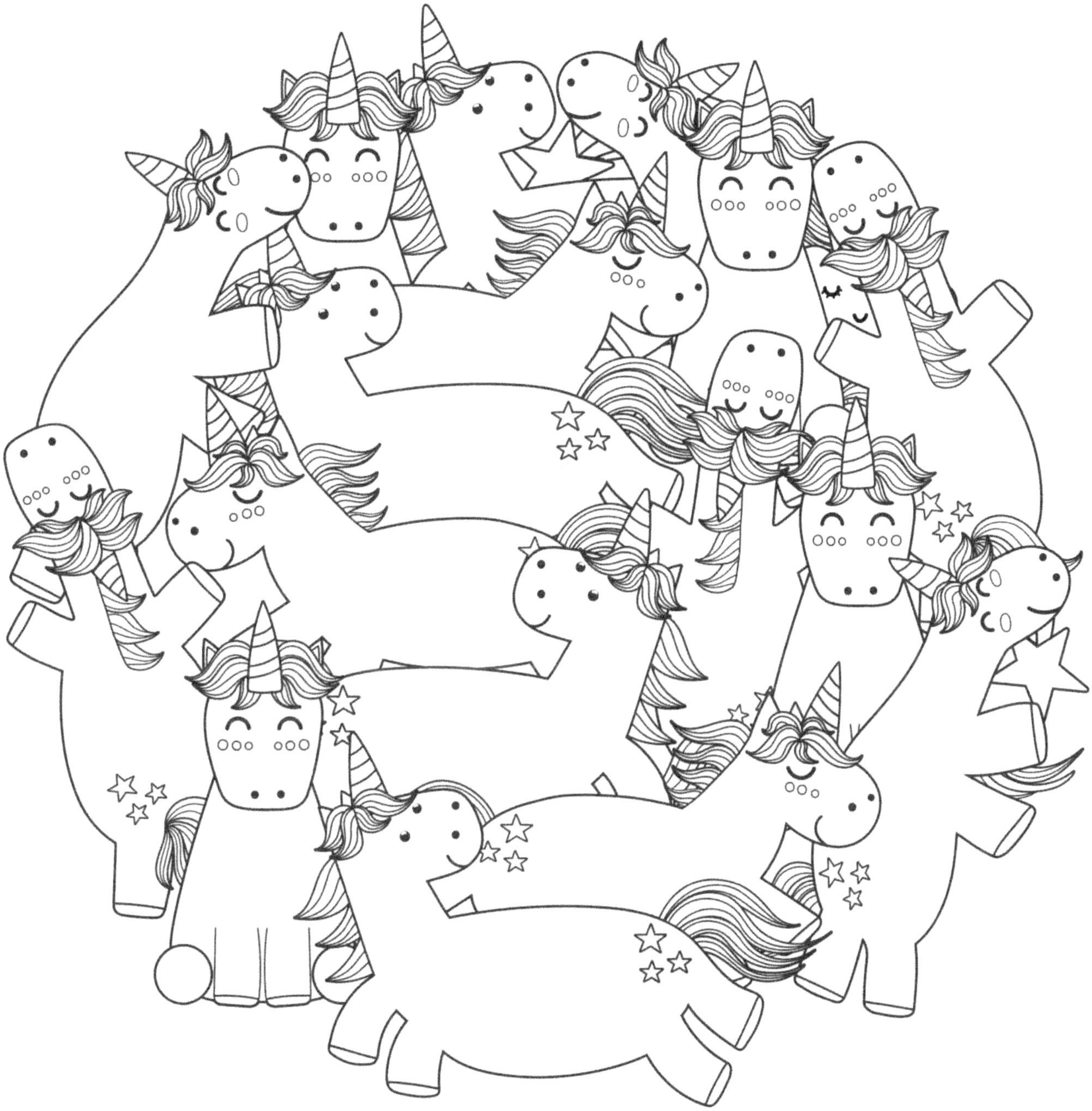

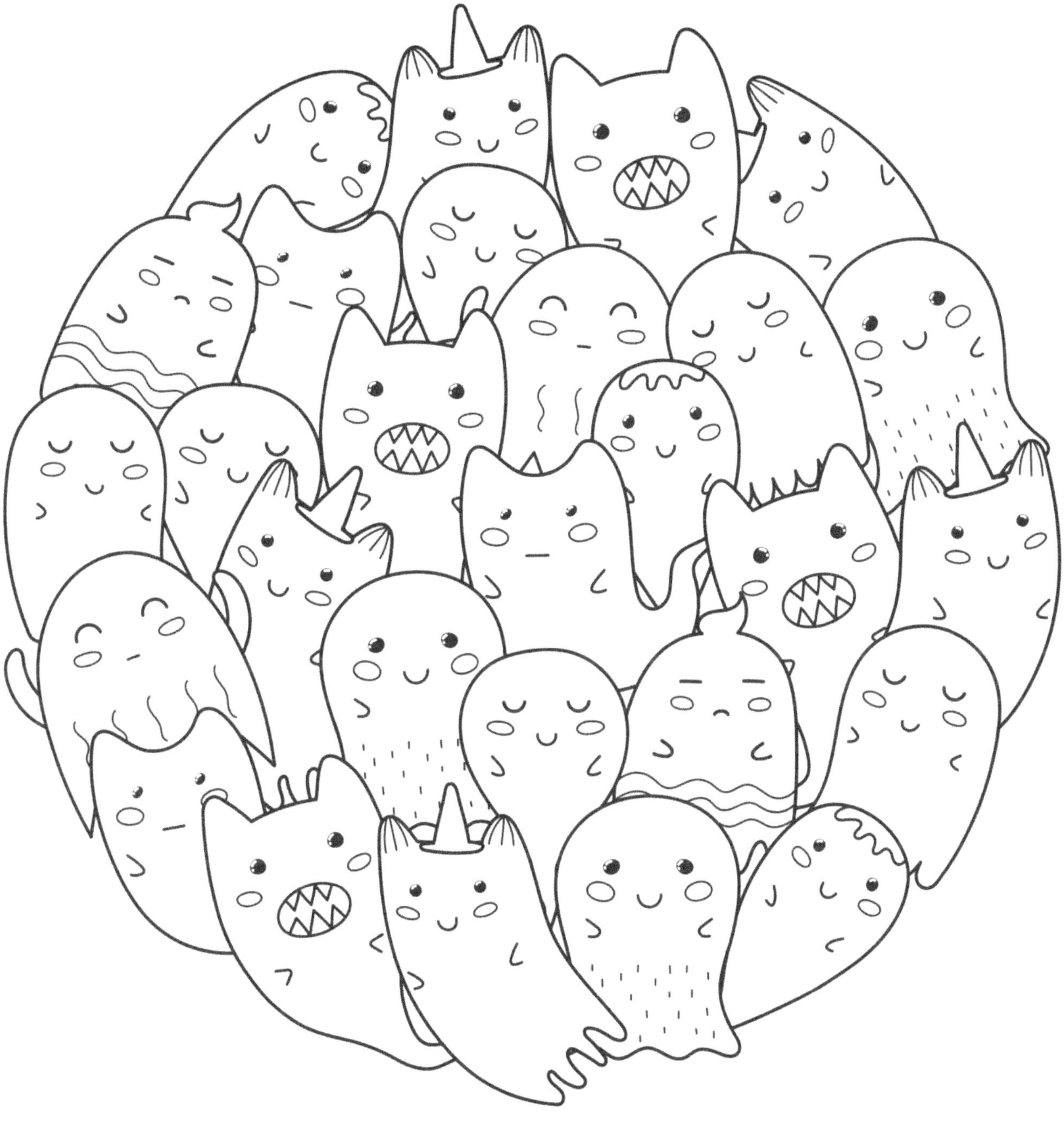

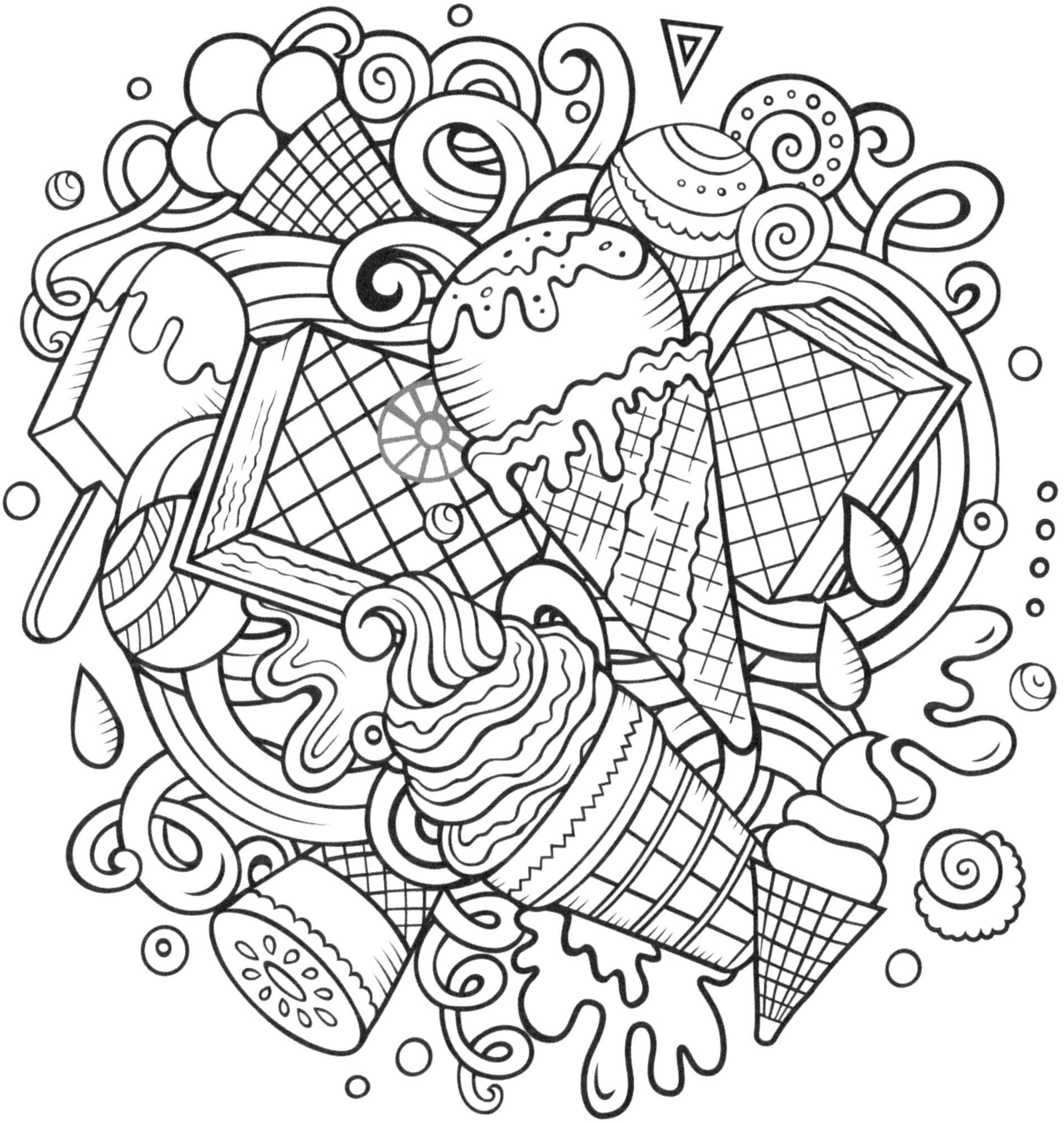

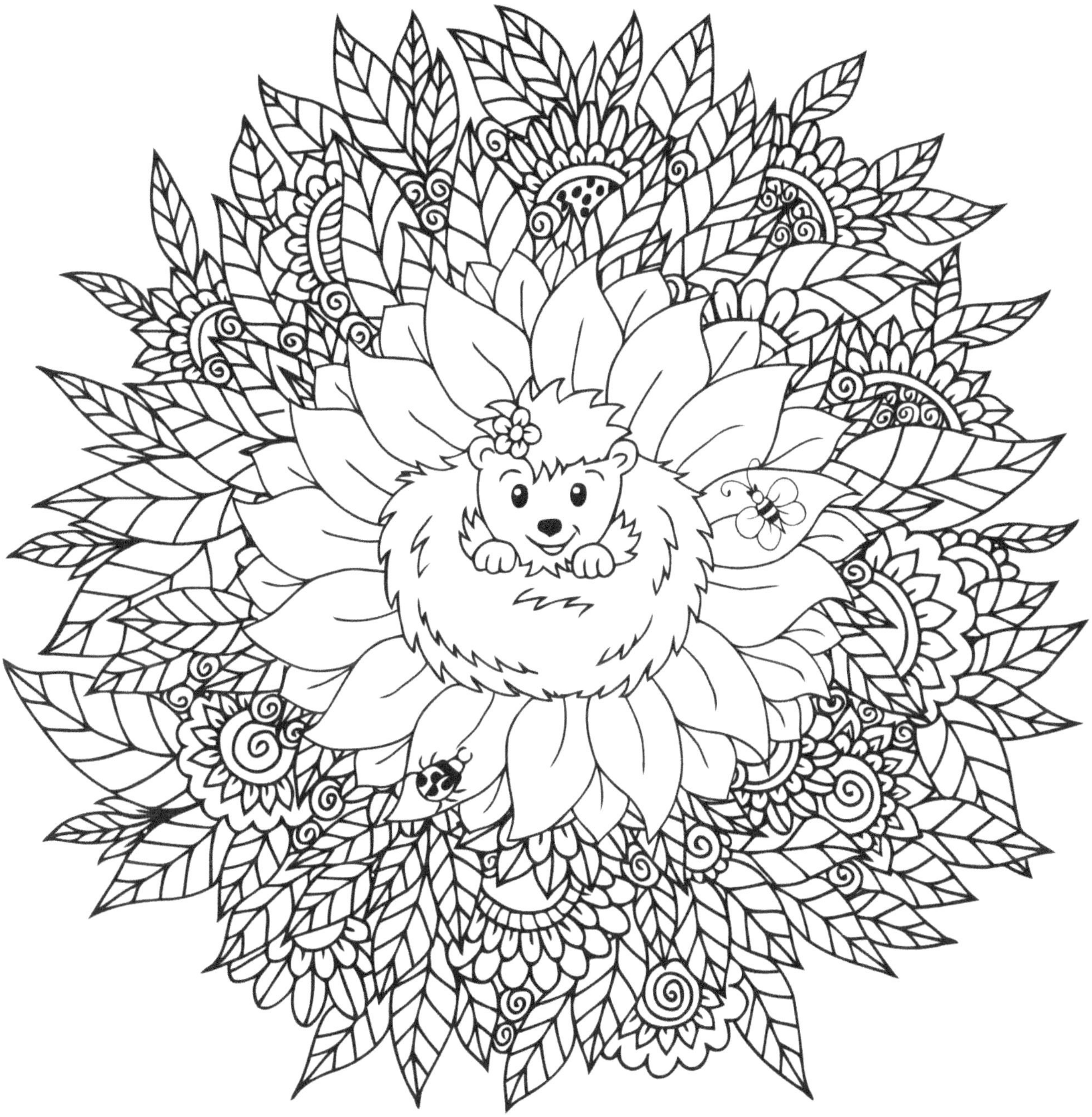

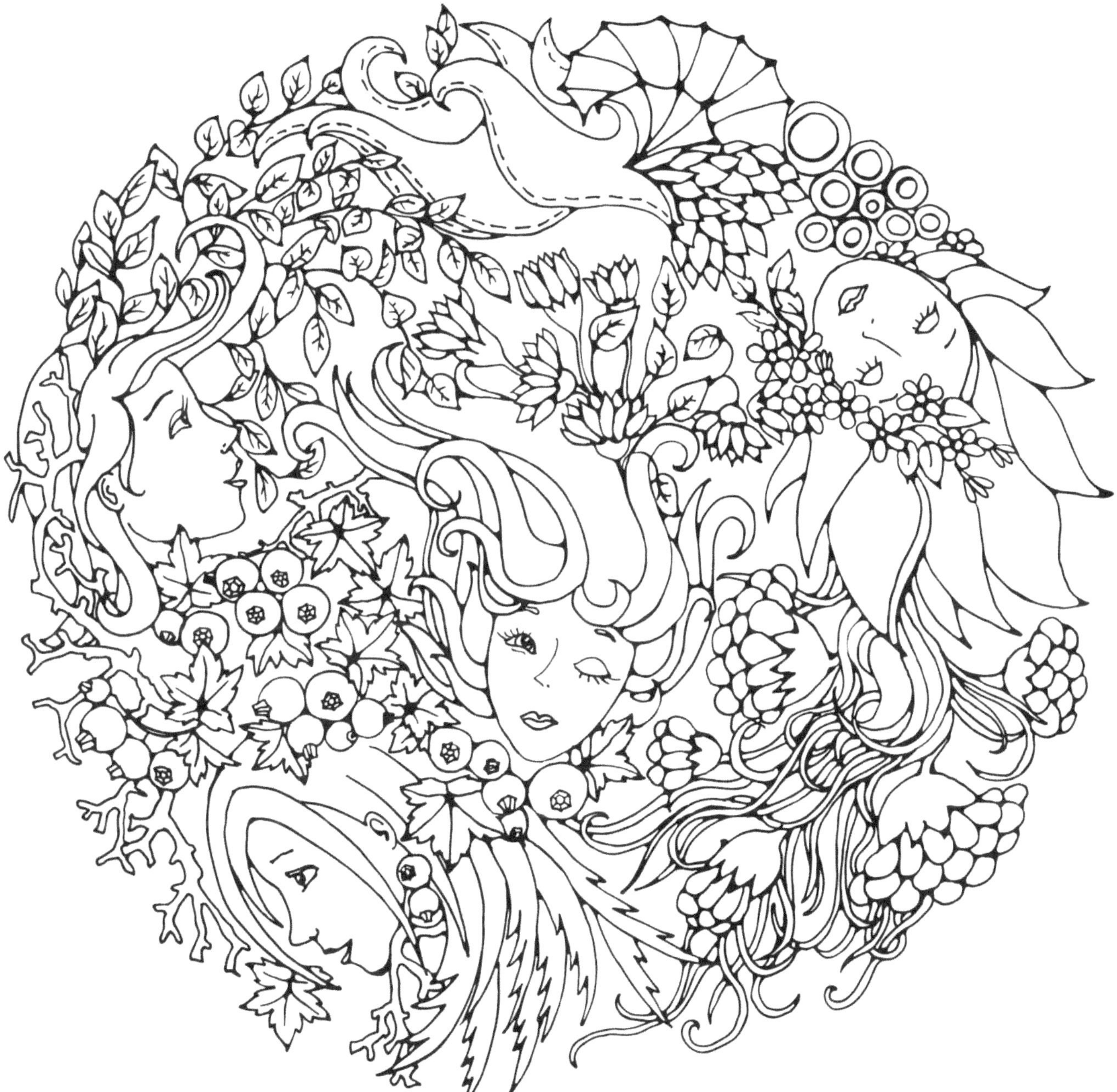

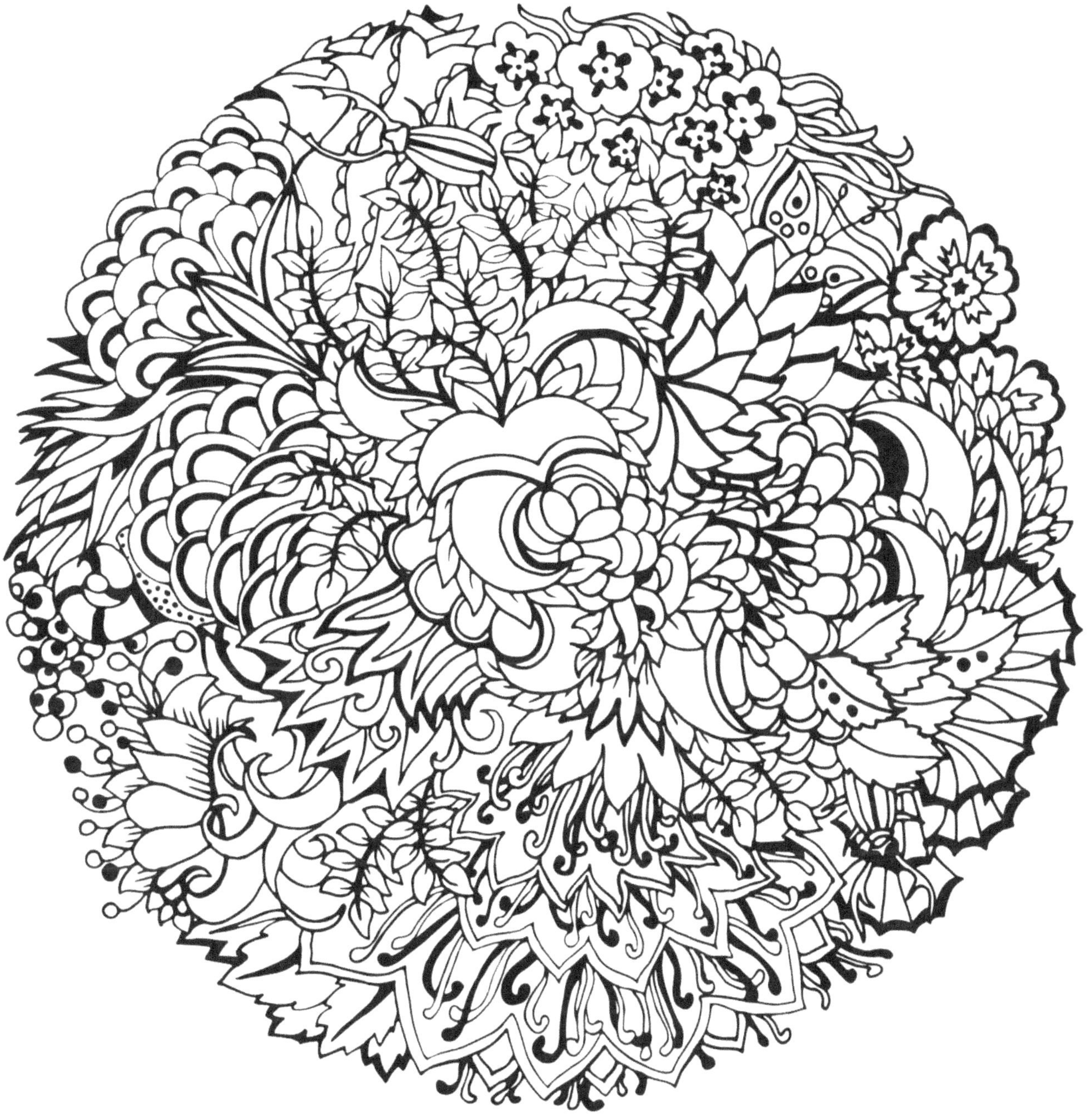

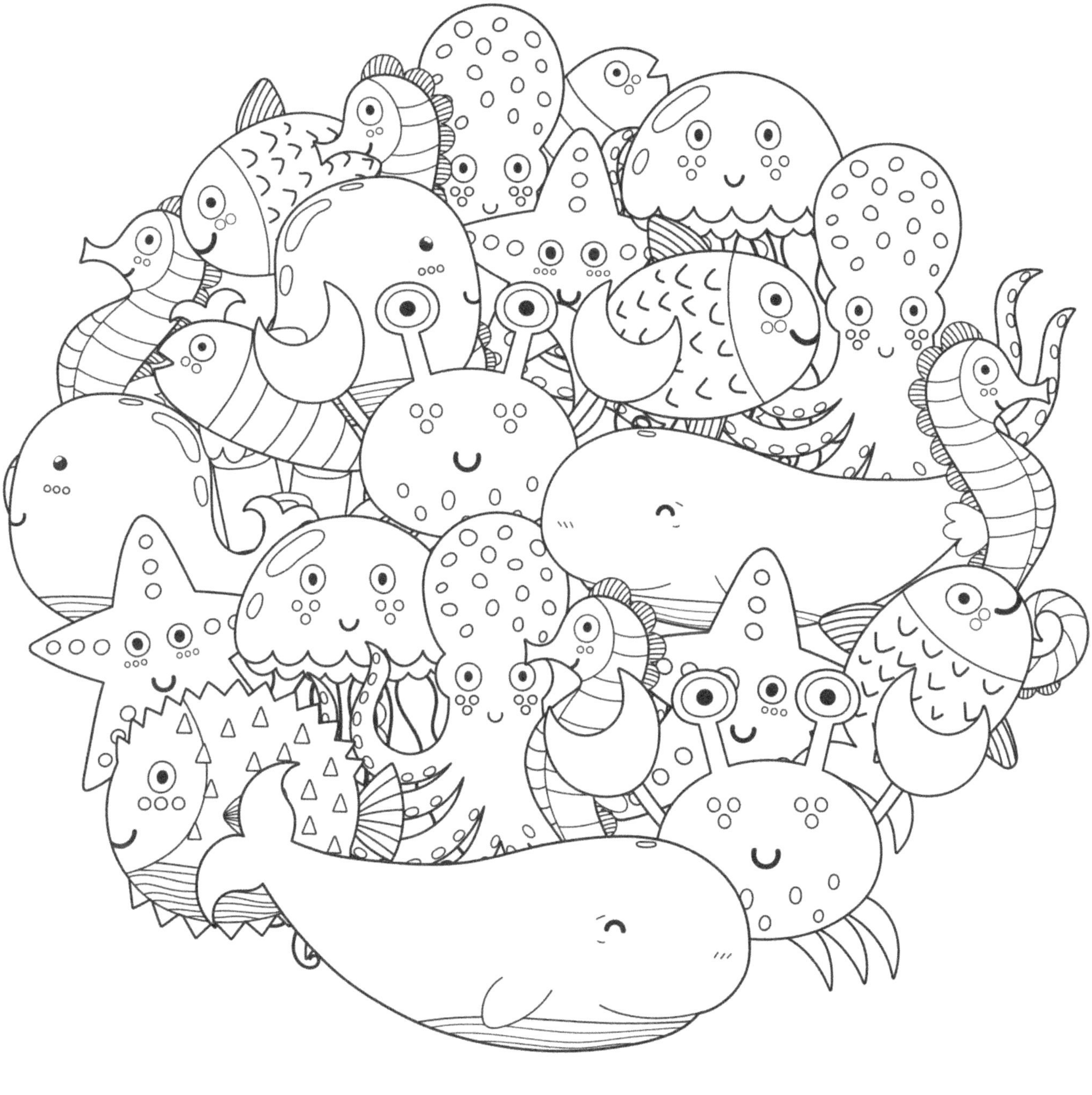

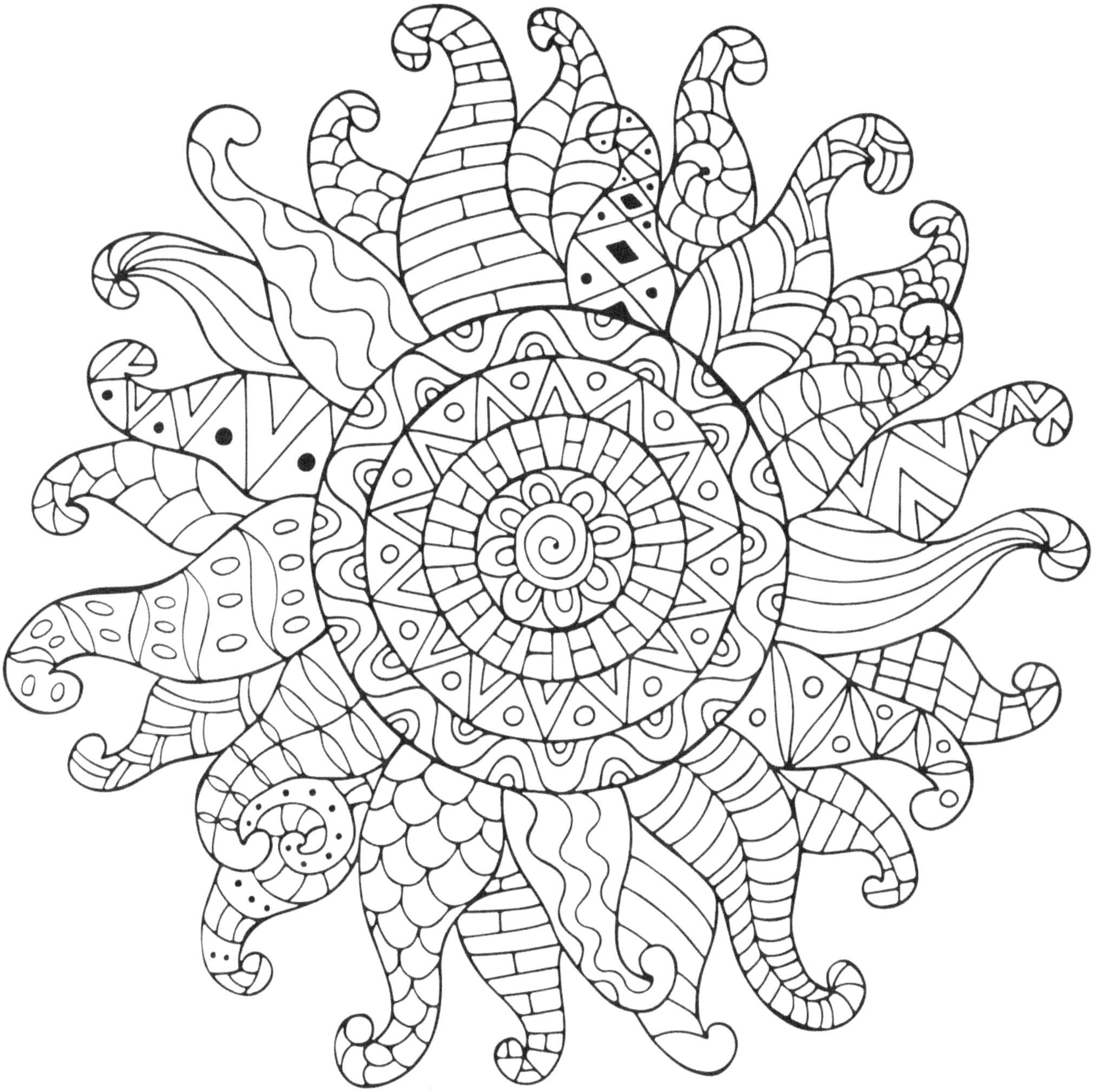

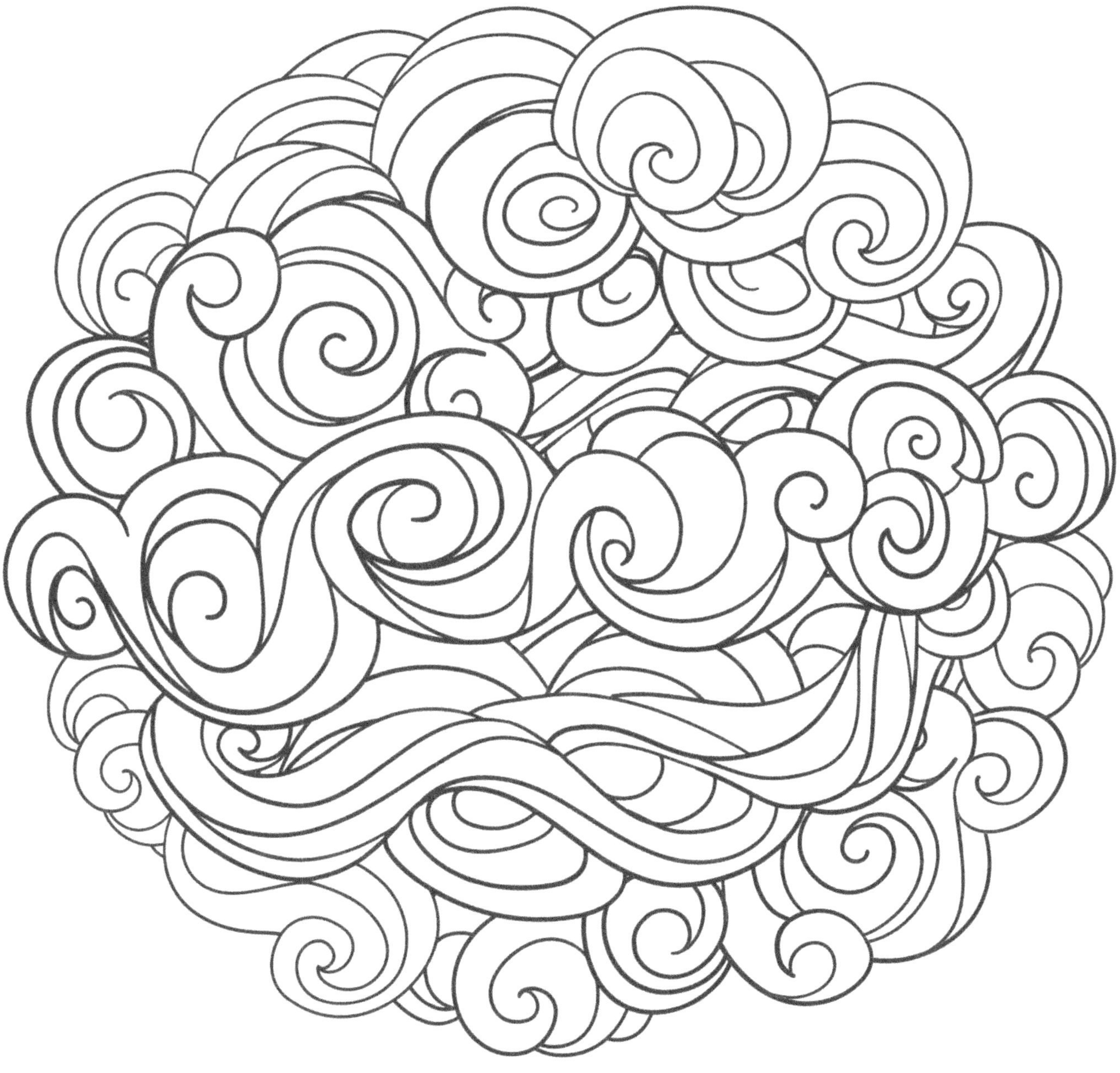

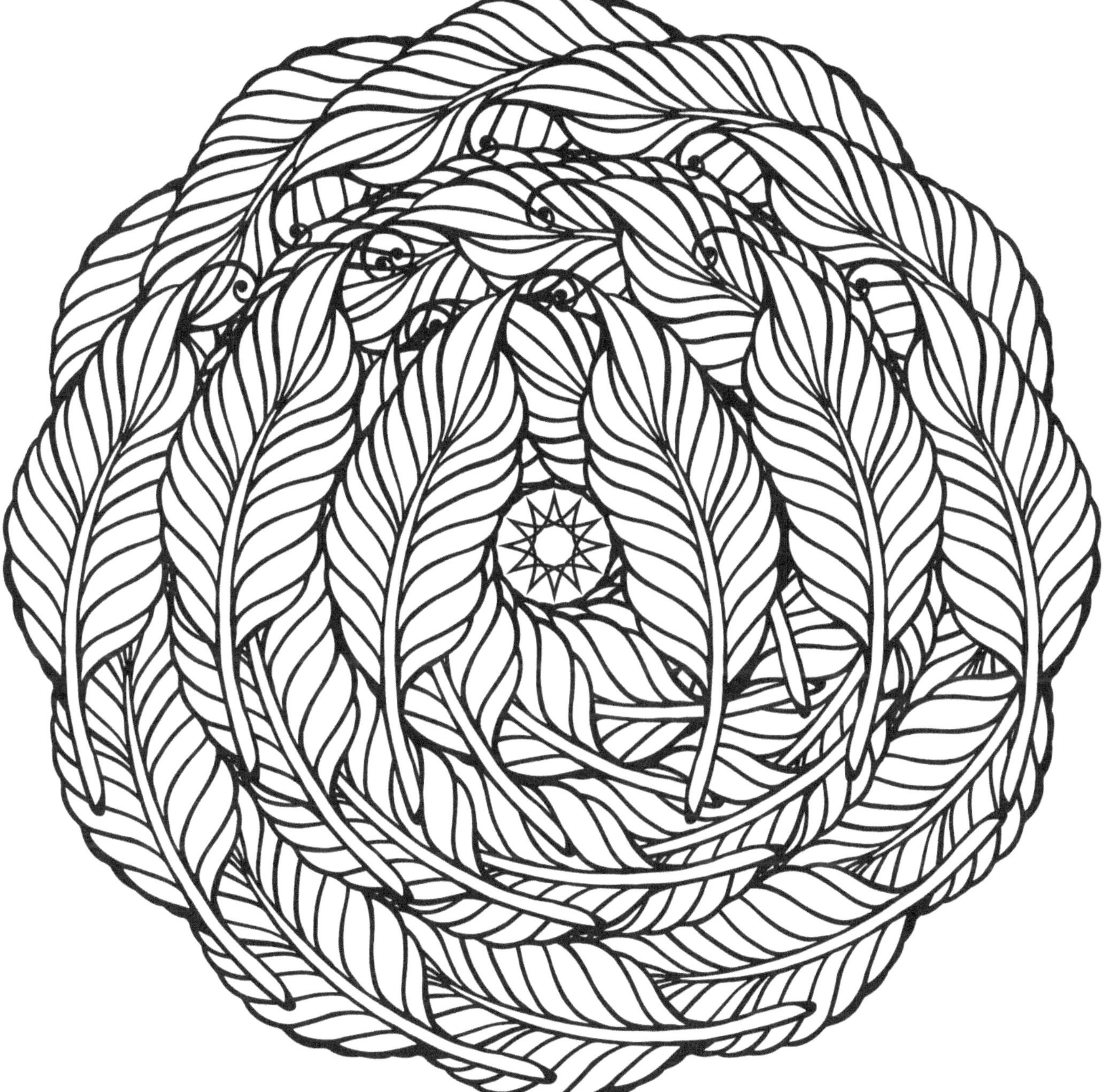

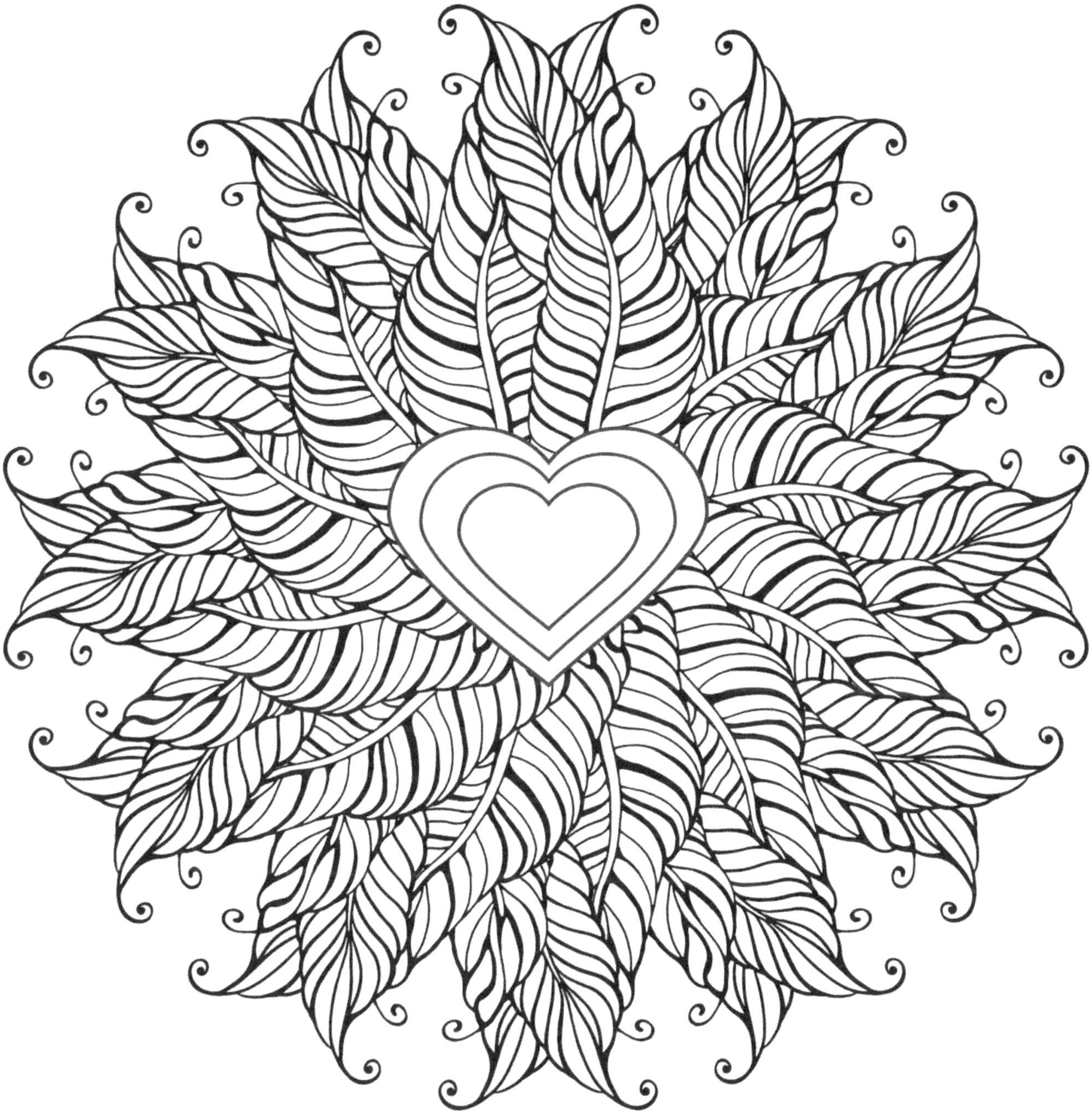

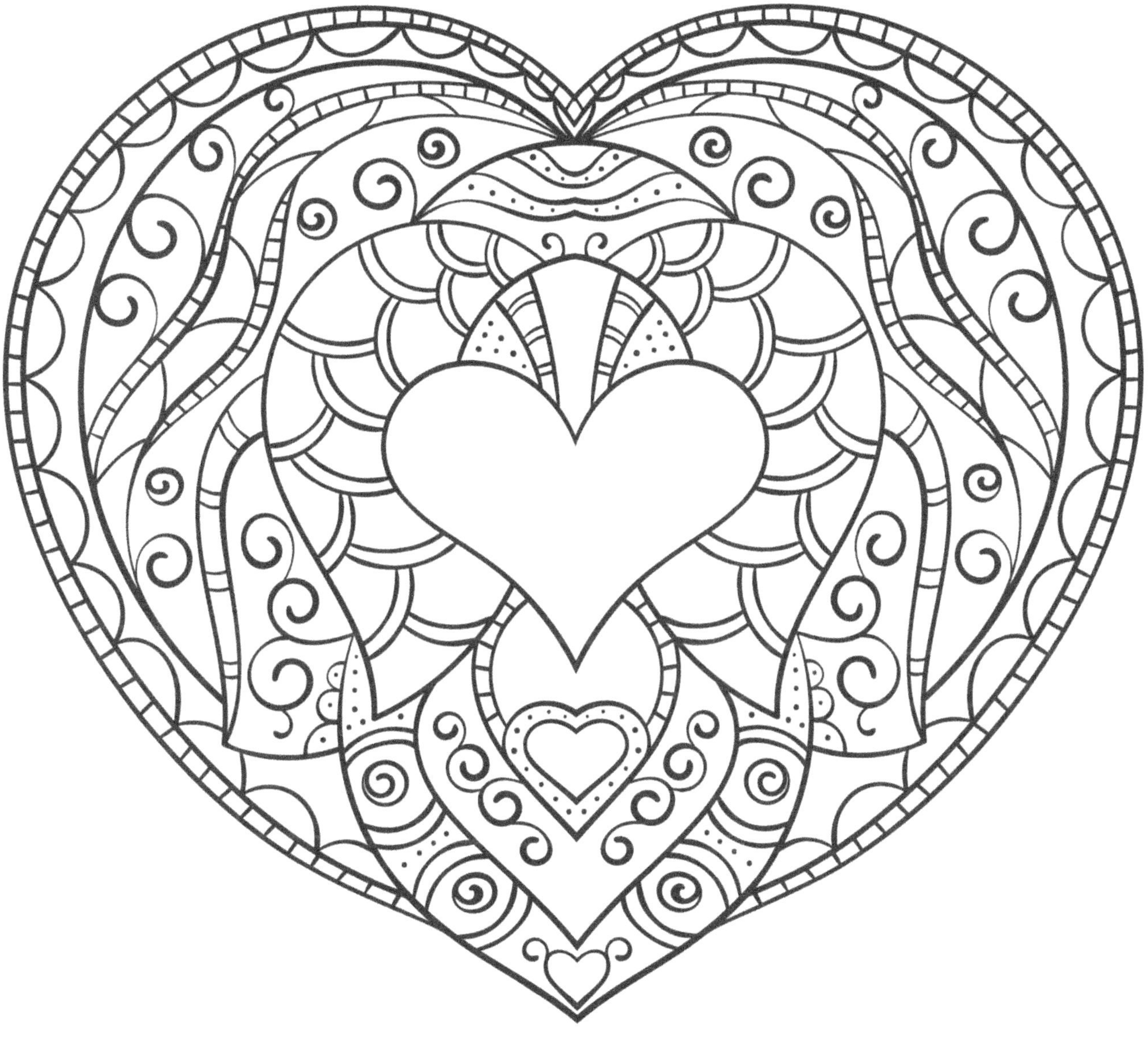

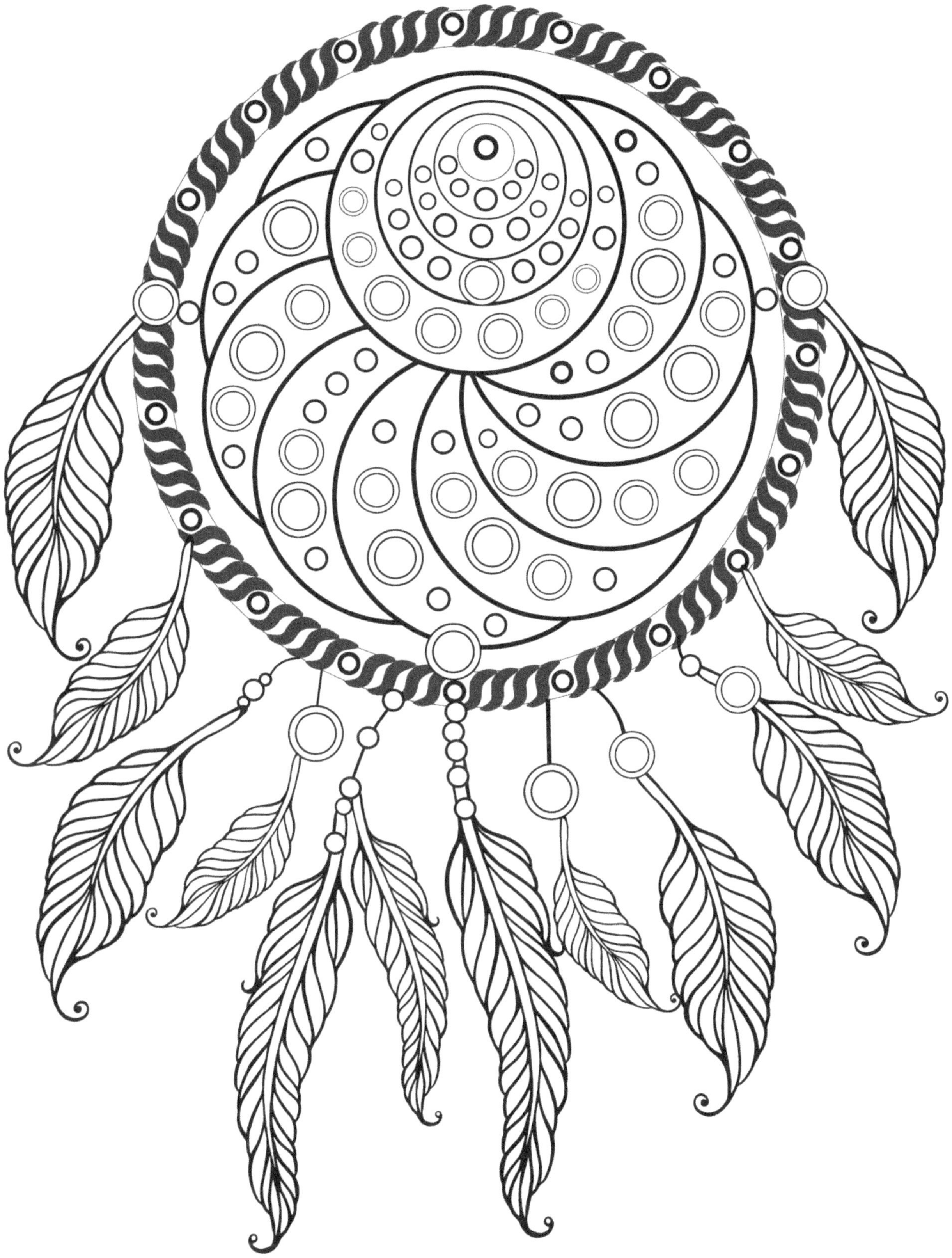

www.ingramcontent.com/pod-product-compliance
Lightning Source LLC
Chambersburg PA
CBHW080138240526
45468CB00009BA/2533
9781974520879